D1714540

Presented to

The Cevens Family

by

The Namgpalra Family

on

2022 - Sept - 11

Published by Candle Books
an imprint of
Lion Hudson plc
Wilkinson House, Jordan Hill Road,
Oxford OX2 8DR, England
www.lionhudson.com/candle

ISBN 978 1 78128 144 4
e-ISBN 978 1 78128 182 6

First edition 2014

A catalogue record for this book is available
from the British Library

Printed and bound in China,
July 2014, LH17

Our Father

Edited by Juliet David
Illustrated by Julie Clay

CANDLE
BOOKS

This simply worded version of the Lord's Prayer
has been specially written to introduce very
young readers to the prayer that Jesus gave us.

It follows closely the words of Scripture in the
Gospel of Matthew, chapter 6 verses 9–13.

This book offers children helpful first steps in
praying the way Jesus taught his followers.

J. D.

One day,
Jesus was praying.

When he finished,
one of his disciples said,
"Lord, teach us to pray."

So Jesus said,
"Pray in this way."

Our Father
in heaven,

help us to
hold your name holy.

Please come and set up
your kingdom.

Then everyone on earth
will obey you –

just as you are obeyed
in heaven.

Give us today
the food
we need.

Forgive us
the wrong things
we have done,

as we forgive others
for the wrong
they have done to us.

Help us
not to give in
when we're tempted.

And protect us
from evil.
Forever,
Amen

BASED ON MATTHEW 6:9–13

Oh, No!

"Food!" said the fly.

"Oh, no!" said the fly.
"Here comes a bird."

"Oh, no!" said the bird.
"Here comes a cat."

The cat said, "Oh, no!
Here comes a dog."

"Oh, no!" said the dog.
"Here comes a woman."

"Oh, no!" said the woman.
"Here comes a fly."

"Food!" said the fly.